THE WEE LITTLE IRISH DRINKING COMPANION

BY
SARAH O'BRIEN

BOTTLED BY

RUNNING PRESS
PHILADELPHIA · LONDON

A Running Press® Miniature Edition™
© 2007 by Running Press
All rights reserved under the Pan-American and International Copyright Conventions
Printed in China

Library of Congress Control Number: 2006925918

ISBN-13: 978-0-7624-2988-2
ISBN-10: 0-7624-2988-7

This book may be ordered by mail from the publisher.
Please include $1.00 for postage and handling.
But try your bookstore first!

Running Press Book Publishers
2300 Chestnut Street, Suite 200
Philadelphia, PA 19103-4371

Visit us on the web!
www.runningpress.com

CONTENTS

12 FL. OZ (355 mL) | ALC. 5.1% / VOL.

INTRODUCTION

It's no secret that drinking is a favorite pastime in the Irish culture. Like the Italians with their pasta and the French with their wine, the Irish have perfected the art of drinking. In Irish culture, drinking and the place of drinking, the pub, has become a way of life. Unlike in America, or other countries where the pub is viewed as a place of revelry, in Ireland, the pub is like a second home. The Irish go there for conversation, atmosphere, company, and the feel of community. It's a wonderful way to get together and socialize with friends and neighbors, and the Irish have managed to turn this pastime into one of the most loved elements of their culture.

To the Irish, drinking is a skill and an art form. Their reputation in this realm is unsurpassed, and you can learn plenty about how to enjoy drinking through this rich tradition. Take it from the Irish: if you drink, do so with friends, do so with gusto, and do so with pride!

IRISH DRINKS

Regardless of your nationality or heritage, the following drinks will imbue you with plenty of Irish spirit in no time.

Irish Beers

If you want to keep things simple, just grab an Irish brewski. Although there are numerous Irish beers, some are more commonly requested, and as a result, most commonly associated with Ireland. This is by no means a comprehensive list, but rather a glimpse into the vast world of Irish beer. Whatever your beer of choice, remember a slow, long swig is the best way to appreciate a fine Irish brew.

Guinness® Stout: To many, this is the quintessential Irish beer and the one most associated with Ireland. A creamy stout with a thick head, many people would argue that a pint of Guinness is the perfect pint.

Harp® Lager: Also brewed by the Guinness company, Harp is a lager with more of a nutty quality.

Beamish® Stout: Another Irish stout, Beamish is not as dry as some of the other stouts. Many people describe it as so creamy and smooth, it is almost milkshake-like in its velvety texture and rich taste.

Smithwicks® Ale (or Kilkenny Irish Cream Ale): This is a type of Irish red ale that gets its red color from the high barley content. This type of beer originated in Ireland and usually has a lower alcohol content than other beers.

Murphy's® Irish Stout: This smooth stout prides itself on being less bitter than its most popular counterpart, Guinness.

Irish Drinks

If you feel up to more of a challenge, try one of the following delicious drink recipes. To make each and every one like a practiced Irishman, here are some handy tips for mixing up the perfect recipe.

Glasses: Use the glass specified in the recipe, or select a glass large enough for the number of ounces that the entire drink recipe will require. To chill a glass, either stick it in the freezer or refrigerator for an hour

or more, or fill the glass with ice and water several minutes before using.

Measuring: If a recipe merely says "part," you can eyeball the measurements by pouring an equal amount of each alcohol into a shot glass. For other measurements, a liquid measuring cup will be quickest and most accurate, or use an ounce shot glass.

Mixing: If a recipe requires shaking, use a cocktail shaker and shake, preferably with ice, before straining into a glass. If a recipe requires only mixing, simply stir with a spoon until the elements are combined. Some recipes may require more than this, so a blender may be desired.

Layering: Keep the elements as separate as possible. Follow the order for pouring ingredients, and pour gently one over the other. If ingredients are still mixing, try pouring layered ingredients over the back of a spoon to keep the pouring gentle and smooth.

Irish Flag

1 part crème de menthe (green)

1 part Baileys® Irish Cream

1 part brandy

First pour the crème de menthe, then the Baileys, and finally the brandy. While pouring into the glass, layer the ingredients so that they don't mix. Once finished, the drink will appear orange, white, and green like the Irish flag.

Irish Sh*tkicker

6 oz. Guinness® beer

6 oz. Harp®

½ oz. Baileys® Irish Cream

½ oz. Irish whiskey

Mix and drink.

Celtic Bull

- 1½ oz. Irish whiskey
- 2 oz. beef bouillon
- 2 oz. tomato juice
- Several dashes Worcestershire sauce
- Dash Tabasco® sauce
- Freshly ground pepper

Mix all ingredients with ice and then combine in a shaker or blender. Pour into a glass and enjoy.

Irish Kiss

1 part Baileys® Irish Cream
1 part peppermint schnapps

Shake with ice and strain into a shot glass.

Grafton Street Sour

1½ oz. Irish whiskey

½ oz. triple sec

1 oz. lime juice

¼ oz. raspberry liqueur

Mix all ingredients, except raspberry liqueur, with ice in a shaker or blender. Strain mixture into a cocktail glass. Top with raspberry liqueur.

Kerry Cooler

2 oz. Irish whiskey
1½ oz. medium sherry
1 oz. orgeat syrup
½ oz. lemon juice
Club soda
Lemon slice

Mix all ingredients, except club soda and lemon slice, with ice in a shaker or blender. Pour into a chilled highball glass and fill with club soda. Garnish with lemon slice.

Irish Shillelagh

1½ oz. Irish whiskey
½ oz. sloe gin
½ oz. light rum
1 oz. lemon juice
1 tsp. sugar syrup
2 peach slices, diced
Fresh raspberries, strawberries,
 or other desired berries
Maraschino cherry

Mix all ingredients, except berries and cherry, in a blender or shaker with ice. Pour into a chilled glass and garnish with berries and cherry.

Paddy Cocktail

- 1½ oz. Irish whiskey
- ¾ oz. sweet vermouth
- Several dashes Angostura® bitters

Mix all ingredients over ice and combine in a shaker or blender. Serve in a chilled glass.

Ring of Kerry

- 1½ oz. Irish whiskey
- 1 oz. Baileys® Irish Cream
- ½ oz. Kahlua®
- 1 tsp. chocolate shavings

Mix all ingredients, except chocolate shavings, with ice in a shaker or blender. Strain into a chilled cocktail glass. Garnish with chocolate shavings.

Shamrock

1½ oz. Irish whiskey

1½ oz. crème de menthe

2 oz. heavy cream

Maraschino cherry

Mix all ingredients, except cherry, with ice in a shaker or blender. Pour into a chilled glass. Garnish with cherry.

Irish Coffee

1½ oz. Irish whiskey

8 oz. hot coffee

1 dash crème de menthe

1 tsp. sugar

Whipped cream

Pour Irish whiskey into a coffee mug, and then add hot coffee and sugar. Stir until sugar is dissolved. Top with whipped cream. Trickle crème de menthe to form green stripes on whipped cream.

Little Leprechaun

| 1 part Irish whiskey

| 1 part Goldschlager® cinnamon schnapps

| 1 part crème de menthe

First pour Irish whiskey into shot glass, then follow with Goldschlager and crème de menthe.

Dublin Driver

| 1 oz. Irish Mist® liqueur
| 3 oz. orange juice

Combine Irish Mist and orange juice over
ice and serve.

Nutty Irishman

| 1 oz. Baileys® Irish Cream
| 1 oz. Frangelico® hazelnut liqueur
| 1 oz. light cream

Pour all ingredients over ice in a shaker and shake until well-mixed. Strain over ice-filled glass.

Little Green Men

½ oz. gin
1½ oz. Jagermeister® liqueur
4 oz. blueberry cocktail mix

Pour gin into glass, then Jagermeister. Fill remaining part of glass with blueberry cocktail mix and watch as your drink turns green.

29

Blackthorn

1½ oz. Irish whiskey

1½ oz. dry vermouth

Several dashes Pernod® licorice liqueur

Several dashes Angostura® bitters

Pour the Irish whiskey, vermouth, Pernod, and bitters over ice into an old-fashioned glass. Stir well and serve.

Killarney

- 1 oz. Irish Mist® liqueur
- 1 oz. gin
- ¾ oz. dry vermouth
- ¼ oz. rosso vermouth
- Slice of lemon

Combine all ingredients with ice in a shaker.
Pour unstrained into an old-fashioned glass.

Add a slice of lemon and serve.

Baby Guinness

2½ oz. Kahlua® coffee liqueur

½ oz. Baileys® Irish Cream

Pour Kahlua into a 3 oz. shot glass, almost filling it. Then, tilt the glass and carefully pour Baileys into the side of the shot glass, giving this "Guinness" its so-called head.

Galway Grey

1½ oz. vodka

1 oz. crème de cacao

1 oz. Cointreau® orange liqueur

½ oz. lime juice

½ oz. light cream

Grated orange peel

Mix all ingredients together, except for cream, and pour into cocktail glass. Pour light cream on top, sprinkle with grated orange peel, and serve.

Southern Ireland

1 part Baileys® Irish Cream
1 part Southern Comfort® peach liqueur

Pour into shot glass and serve.

Emerald Isle

2 oz. gin
1 tsp. green crème de menthe
3 dashes Angostura® bitters

Combine all ingredients with ice, strain into cocktail glass, and serve.

Everybody's Irish

1½ oz. Irish whiskey
¾ oz. crème de menthe (green)
¾ oz. green Chartreuse®

Stir into a cocktail glass and serve.

Irish Catholic

¾ oz. Irish whiskey
¼ oz. amaretto almond liqueur

Pour into a shot glass and serve.

Irish Kilt

2 oz. Irish whiskey

1 oz. scotch

1 oz. lemon juice

1 oz. sugar water

3 dashes orange bitters

Combine all the ingredients in a shaker filled with ice, shake well, and strain into a cocktail glass.

Morning with Leprechauns

1½ oz. Baileys® Irish Cream

1 oz. Irish whiskey

¼ oz. cherry brandy

3 oz. cold, black coffee

Combine all the ingredients into a highball glass filled with crushed ice and stir.

Blarney Stone

1½ to 2 oz. Irish whiskey

½ tsp. Pernod®

½ tsp. curaçao

½ tsp. maraschino liqueur

Dash Angostura® bitters

½ cup crushed ice

Twist orange peel

Olive

Mix all ingredients, except the orange peel and olive, in a shaker and shake well. Strain into a cocktail glass and garnish with the peel and olive.

DRINKING QUOTES

While mixing your drinks, remember you're in great company. Whether born with Irish blood or not, these individuals show a skill with the art of drinking that makes them honorary Irishmen. From Mark Twain to Humphrey Bogart, all the great ones have some words—whether witty, celebratory, or just downright frank— that speak to the drinker in all of us.

The problem with some people is that when they aren't drunk, they're sober.

—WILLIAM BUTLER YEATS

A drink a day keeps the shrink away.

—EDWARD ABBEY

Give an Irishman lager for a month and he's a dead man. An Irishman's stomach is lined with copper, and the beer corrodes it. But whiskey polishes the copper and is the saving of him.

—MARK TWAIN

I envy people who drink. At least they have something to blame everything on.

—OSCAR LEVANT

Give me a woman who loves beer and I will conquer the world.

—KAISER WELHELM

Always do sober what you said you'd do drunk. That will teach you to keep your mouth shut.

—ERNEST HEMINGWAY

I drink to make other people interesting.

—GEORGE JEAN NATHAN

Work is the curse of the drinking class.

—OSCAR WILDE

Only Irish coffee provides in a single glass all four essential food groups: alcohol, caffeine, sugar, and fat.

—ALEX LEVINE

I'll have what the man on the floor is having!

—ANONYMOUS

The problem with the world is that everyone is a few drinks behind.

—HUMPHREY BOGART

It only takes one drink to get me drunk. The trouble is, I can't remember if it's the thirteenth or the fourteenth.

—GEORGE BURNS

When I read about the evils of drinking, I gave up reading.

—HENNY YOUNGMAN

You're not drunk if you can lie on the floor without holding on.

—DEAN MARTIN

I distrust camels and anyone else who can go a week without a drink.

—JOE E. LEWIS

Reality is an illusion that occurs due to the lack of alcohol.

—Anonymous

Eat thy bread with joy, and drink thy wine with a merry heart.

—Ecclesiastes 9:7

A mouth of a perfectly happy man is filled with beer.

—Ancient Egyptian Wisdom, 2200 b.c.

First you take a drink, then the drink takes a drink, then the drink takes you.

—Francis Scott Key Fitzgerald

If drinking is interfering with your work, you're probably a heavy drinker. If work is interfering with your drinking, you're probably an alcoholic.

—ANONYMOUS

Alcohol may be man's worst enemy, but the Bible says love your enemy.

—FRANK SINATRA

What whiskey will not cure, there is no cure for.

—IRISH PROVERB

What contemptible scoundrel has stolen the cork to my lunch?

—W.C. FIELDS

Beer makes you feel the way you ought to feel without beer.

—HENRY LAWSON

A hangover is the wrath of grapes.

—ANONYMOUS

Even though a number of people have tried, no one has ever found a way to drink for a living.

—JEAN KERR

TOASTS AND BLESSINGS

Once you have your Irish drinks mixed, you still need to learn to drink like an Irishman. For starters, every drink that a true Irishman takes has a toast to go along with it, whether at a wedding, baptism, sporting event, or among friends. If you plan to drink with an Irishman, have a toast or a blessing memorized.

Here's to cheating, stealing,
fighting, and drinking.
If you cheat, cheat death.
If you steal, steal a woman's heart.
If you fight, fight for a brother.
If you drink, drink with me!

May the roof above us never fall in,
and may the friends gathered below it
never fall out.

The horse and mule live thirty years
And never know of wines and beers.
The goat and sheep at twenty die
Without a taste of scotch or rye.
The cow drinks water by the ton
And at eighteen is mostly done.
The dog at fifteen cashes in
Without the aid of rum or gin.
The modest, sober, bone-dry hen
Lays eggs for noggs and dies at ten.
But sinful, ginful, rum-soaked men
Survive three-score years and ten.
And some of us . . . though mighty few
Stay pickled 'til we're ninety-two.

There are several good reasons for drinking
and one has just entered my head.

If a man can't drink when he's living,
then how the heck can he drink
when he's dead!

May the devil make a ladder of your backbone
while he is picking apples in the garden of Hell.

Wherever you go and whatever you do,
may the luck of the Irish be there with you.

May the leprechauns be near you,
to spread luck along your way.
And may all the Irish angels
smile on you St. Patrick's Day.

Here's to a long life and a merry one.

A quick death and an easy one.

A pretty girl and an honest one.

A cold beer—and another one!

In heaven there is no beer . . .
That's why we drink ours here.

May the Good Lord take
a liking to you . . . but not
too soon!

An Irishman is never drunk as
long as he can hold onto one
blade of grass and not fall off
the face of the earth.

Some Guinness was spilt on the barroom floor

When the pub was shut for the night.

When out of his hole crept a wee brown mouse

And stood in the pale moonlight.

He lapped up the frothy foam from the floor

Then back on his haunches he sat.

And all night long, you could hear the
mouse roar,

"Bring on the goddamn cat!"

The greatest love—the love above all loves,

Even greater than that of a mother . . .

Is the tender, passionate, undying love,

Of one beer drunken slob for another.

May your glass be ever full. May the roof
over your head be always strong. And may
you be in heaven half an hour before the
devil knows you're dead.

May there always be work for your hands to do,

May your purse always hold a coin or two.

May the sun always shine

warm on your windowpane,

May a rainbow be certain to follow each rain.

May the hand of a friend always be near you,

And may God fill your heart

with gladness to cheer you.

When money's tight and hard to get
and your horse is also ran,
When all you have is a heap of debt
a pint of plain is your only man.

As you slide down the banister of life,

May the splinters never point the wrong way.

If you're lucky enough to be
Irish ... You're lucky enough!

May you live as long as you
want, and never want as long
as you live.

There are only two kinds
of people in the world:
the Irish and those
who wish they were.

Always remember to forget
The troubles that passed away.
But never forget to remember
The blessings that come each day.

Nary a day goes by that I miss to wonder why
the moon shows his face as the day draws nigh.
In the firelight I ponder my canine's thought
as he gazes upon me from his hand-me-down cot.
I think of God and all his creations,
one being the women with their
unbridled temptations.
I have searched for love with no direction,
skeletons in the closet . . . a fine collection.
These quandaries of mine, I'm sure to figure out.
For I know the answer lies
at the bottom of this stout.

'Tis better to buy a small bouquet
And give to your friend this very day,
Than a bushel of roses white and red
To lay on his coffin after he's dead.

What is Irish diplomacy?

It's the ability to tell a man
to go to hell,

So that he will look forward
to making the trip.

Health and a long life to you.
Land without rent to you.
A child every year to you.
And if you can't go to heaven,
May you at least die in Ireland.

May the road rise to meet you.

May the wind be always at your back.

May the sun shine warm upon your face.

And rains fall soft upon your fields.

And until we meet again,

May God hold you

in the hollow of His hand.

May your troubles be less
and your blessings be more.
And nothing but happiness
come through your door.

May the winds of fortune sail you,
May you sail a gentle sea.
May it always be the other guy
who says, "this drink's on me."

Ireland, it's the one place on earth
That heaven has kissed
With melody, mirth,
And meadow and mist.

May your Guardian Angel be at your side
to pick ya up off the floor
and hand ya another cold stout
from the store.

Of all my favorite things to do,
the utmost is to have a brew.
My love grows for my foamy friend,
with each thirst-quenching elbow bend.
Beer's so frothy, smooth, and cold—
It's paradise—pure liquid gold.
Yes, beer means many things to me . . .
That's all for now, I gotta pee!

A boy may kiss his girl goodbye,

The sun may kiss the butterfly,

The wine may kiss the crystal glass,

And you, my friend, may kiss my ass.

May you live to be a hundred years,

With one extra year to repent!

Sláinte!

(Pronounced "slawn-cha," meaning "Health!" This is a common toast in Ireland, similar to "Cheers.")

IRISH DRINKING SONGS

You don't have to be Irish to belt out a drunken tune, but the Irish are quite the experts. As with toasts, an Irishman always has a song ready (even if the lyrics come out a bit slurred). Just in case you can't understand a slurred Irish tune, here are the lyrics to some of the most popular drinking songs.

Whiskey in the Jar

As I was going over
the far famed Kerry mountains,

I met with Captain Farrell,
and his money he was counting.

I first produced my pistol,
and I then produced my rapier.

Sayin' stand and deliver,
for I am a bold deceiver.

Chorus

Musha ring dumma do damma da

Whack for the daddy 'ol

Whack for the daddy 'ol

There's whiskey in the jar

I counted out his money,
and it made a pretty penny.

I put it in my pocket
and I took it home to Jenny.

She sighed and she swore
that she never would deceive me,

but the Devil take the women,
for they never can be easy.

Chorus

I went into my chamber,
all for to take a slumber,

I dreamt of gold and jewels
and for sure it was no wonder.

But Jenny drew my charges
and she filled them up with water,

Then sent for Captain Farrell
to be ready for the slaughter.

Chorus

T'was early in the morning,
    just before I rose to travel,

Up comes a band of footmen
and likewise Captain Farrell.

I first produced my pistol,
for she'd stolen away my rapier,

But I couldn't shoot the water
so a prisoner I was taken.

Chorus

Now there's some take delight
in the carriages a-rollin',

And others take delight
in the hurley and the bowlin'.

But I take delight
in the juice of the barley,

And courting pretty fair maids
in the morning bright and early.

Chorus

If anyone can aid me,
'tis my brother in the army,

If I can find his station
in Cork or in Killarney.

And if he'll go with me,
we'll go roving in Kilkenny,

And I'm sure he'll treat me better
than me darling sportling Jenny.

Chorus

Four Green Fields

What did I have, said the fine old woman,

What did I have, this proud old woman did say.

I had four green fields, each one was a jewel,

But strangers came
and tried to take them from me.

I had fine strong sons,
who fought to save my jewels.

They fought and they died,
and that was my grief, said she.

Long time ago, said the fine old woman,

Long time ago,
this proud old woman did say,

There was war and death,
plundering and pillage.

My children starved,
by mountain, valley and sea,

And their wailing cries,
they shook the very heavens.

My four green fields
ran red with their blood, said she.

What have I now,
said the fine old woman,

What have I now,
this proud old woman did say,

I have four green fields,
one of them's in bondage

In stranger's hands,
that tried to take it from me,

But my sons had sons,
as brave as were their fathers,

My fourth green field
will bloom once again, said she.

The Irish National Anthem

The Soldier's Song!
We'll sing a song, a soldier's song,
With cheering rousing chorus,
As 'round our blazing fires we throng,
The starry heavens o'er us;
Impatient for the coming fight,
And as we wait the morning's light,
Here in the silence of the night,
We'll chant a soldier's song.

Chorus
Soldiers are we
Whose lives are pledged to Ireland;
Some have come
From a land beyond the wave.

Sworn to be free,
No more our ancient sire land
Shall shelter the despot or the slave.
Tonight we man the gap of danger
In Erin's cause, come woe or weal
'Mid cannons' roar and rifles peal,
We'll chant a soldier's song.

In valley green, on towering crag,
Our fathers fought before us,
And conquered 'neath the same old flag
That's proudly floating o'er us.
We're children of a fighting race,
That never yet has known disgrace,
And as we march, the foe to face,
We'll chant a soldier's song.

Chorus

Sons of the Gael! Men of the Pale!
The long watched day is breaking;
The serried ranks of Inisfail
Shall set the Tyrant quaking.
Our campfires now are burning low;
See in the east a silv'ry glow,
Out yonder waits the Saxon foe,
So chant a soldier's song.

Chorus

The Wild Rover

I've been a wild rover for many a year

And I spent all my money
on whiskey and beer,

And now I'm returning
with gold in great store

And I never will play the wild rover no more.

Chorus

And it's no, nay, never,

No nay never no more,

Will I play the wild rover

No never no more.

I went to an alehouse I used to frequent

And I told the landlady my money was spent.

I asked her for credit, she answered me, "Nay

Such a custom as yours I could have any day."

Chorus

I took from my pocket ten sovereigns bright

And the landlady's eyes
opened wide with delight.

She said, "I have whiskey, and wines of the best

And the words that I spoke
sure were only in jest."

Chorus

I'll go home to my parents,
confess what I've done

And I'll ask them to pardon their prodigal son.

And if they caress (forgive) me,
as ofttimes before

Sure I never will play the wild rover no more.

Chorus

Danny Boy

Oh Danny boy, the pipes, the pipes are calling

From glen to glen,
and down the mountain side.

The summer's gone,
and all the flowers are dying
'Tis you, 'tis you must go and I must bide.

But come ye back
when summer's in the meadow

Or when the valley's hushed
and white with snow.
'Tis I'll be here in sunshine or in shadow,

Oh Danny boy, oh Danny boy, I love you so.

And if you come,
when all the flowers are dying

And I am dead, as dead I well may be,

You'll come and find
the place where I am lying,

And kneel and say an "Ave" there for me.

And I shall hear, tho' soft you tread above me,

And all my dreams will warm and sweeter be.

If you'll not fail to tell me that you love me,

I'll simply sleep in peace until you come to me.

I'll simply sleep in peace until you come to me.

Dirty Old Town

I found my love by the gasworks croft
Dreamed a dream by the old canal
Kissed my girl by the factory wall
Dirty old town, dirty old town.

Clouds are drifting across the moon
Cats are prowling on their beat
Spring's a girl in the street at night
Dirty old town, dirty old town.

I heard a siren from the docks
Saw a train set the night on fire
Smelled the spring in the smokey wind
Dirty old town, dirty old town.

I'm going to make a good sharp axe
Shining steel tempered in the fire
We'll chop you down like an old dead tree
Dirty old town, dirty old town.

When Irish Eyes Are Smiling

There's a tear in your eye,
And I'm wondering why,
For it never should be there at all.
With such pow'r in your smile,
Sure a stone you'd beguile,
So there's never a teardrop should fall
When your sweet lilting laughter's
Like some fairy song,
And your eyes twinkle bright as can be;
You should laugh all the while
And all other times smile,
And now, smile a smile for me.

Chorus

When Irish eyes are smiling,
Sure, 'tis like the morn in Spring.
In the lilt of Irish laughter
You can hear the angels sing.
When Irish hearts are happy,
All the world seems bright and gay.
And when Irish eyes are smiling,
Sure, they steal your heart away.

For your smile is a part
Of the love in your heart,
And it makes even sunshine more bright.
Like the linnet's sweet song,
Crooning all the day long,
Comes your laughter and light.
For the springtime of life
Is the sweetest of all
There is ne'er a real care or regret;
And while springtime is ours
Throughout all of youth's hours,
Let us smile each chance we get.

Chorus

HANGOVER CURES

No drinking companion would be complete without addressing that unfortunate side effect of the drink, the dreaded hangover. While studies have shown that there is no scientific hangover cure, this hasn't stopped people from marketing their one tried and true method. The following are some of the most common "cures" for the hangover.

The Hair of the Dog

Only the most hardcore drinkers believe in the old "hair of the dog" practice. The thinking behind this "cure" is that your body can't be hungover while it is still consuming alcohol, which requires you to start drinking as soon as you wake up in the morning. However, all this does is put off the hangover until a little bit longer.

Water

Since alcohol is a diuretic, the main cause of a hangover is dehydration, so naturally, you need to replenish your body's lost fluids. Hydrate, hydrate, hydrate. What's even better is drinking a glass of water before you go to bed, but chances are you weren't thinking straight to begin with, so fat chance of that happening.

Caffeine

For some reason, many people rush to grab a coffee, coke, or any other form of caffeine to help them deal with that pounding headache that accompanies a hangover. Although caffeine may temporarily relieve your headache, like alcohol, it also dehydrates you. If you do swear by a large, black coffee, make sure you're also drinking plenty of water.

Ginger

Ginger is a popular hangover cure because of its ability to relieve an upset stomach—a common symptom of the hangover. Many consume it in the form of tea, but any form will do.

Greasy Food

Strangely enough, greasy food seems to hit the spot and relieve some of the symptoms associated with hangovers. Whether it's pizza, burgers, French fries, or chicken wings, hurting, hung-over souls tend to gravitate toward this grub. Some believe the grease absorbs the alcohol, relieving some of the symptoms, but no one really knows for sure how, why, or if it actually works.

Tomato Juice/Vegetable Juice/Bloody Mary

Ahh, the infamous morning-after drink—the Bloody Mary. Tomato or vegetable juice provides the body with many vitamins and minerals lost during a hard night of drinking. If you're so inclined, mix up a Bloody Mary and get back in the game, or omit the vodka and have a nutritious, start-the-day beverage.

Bloody Mary

1½ – 2 oz. vodka

4 oz. tomato juice

1 tsp. Worcestershire sauce

1 tsp. lemon juice

Tabasco® sauce and pepper to taste

Stalk of celery

Pour over ice and add a stalk of celery to garnish.